pilates

ON THE ball

training core stability for
a healthy body and mind

pilates
ON THE ball

training core stability for
a healthy body and mind

Gemma Wright

p

This is a Parragon Publishing Book
First published in 2006

Parragon Publishing
Queen Street House
4 Queen Street
Bath BA1 1HE, UK

ISBN: 1-40547-122-0

Printed in China

Created and produced by THE BRIDGEWATER BOOK COMPANY

Photography: Ian Parsons
Models: Zoë Hubbard and Gemma Wright

Caution
Please check with your doctor/therapist before attempting this workout,
particularly if you are suffering from an injury, are pregnant, or have just
had a baby. It is recommended that new mothers wait at least six weeks
post partum before participating in exercise (12 weeks if it was a cesarean
birth). If you feel any pain or discomfort at any point, please stop
exercising immediately and seek medical advice.

contents

introduction

Pilates on the ball combines the two most effective core-stability training systems into one fantastic workout. You'll gain the benefits of Pilates added to the fun of working out on the Swiss Ball—two for the price of one! Whether you are a total novice, an experienced exerciser, or an elite athlete, this is a workout you can do, and will enjoy.

What is core stability?

Core stability is the focus in fitness today, but what is it? Core stability equals a strong inner unit, i.e. the deep muscles that lie closest to the spine. If we can develop a strong inner core, the outer unit is able to move with more ease and efficiency—similar to the roots of a tree, which allow the trunk and branches of the tree to move freely in the wind. If the roots of the tree are weak, the tree will blow over in a storm, but if they are strong, they will hold the tree firmly in place. Do you find it difficult to hold yourself sitting upright for very long? Do you begin to slouch and round your back? If the answer is yes, your core stability could be weak. Core stability is about building strength from within—without it, muscle imbalances and, in turn, back pain can result. It is essential for better posture and improved all-round function in our daily lives.

Pilates and the Swiss Ball have been brought together in this book to create a challenging, effective, and fun workout, suitable for everybody, which will focus on strengthening your core. Using the ball to perform Pilates exercises can take your workout to a new level by providing a variety of movement and adding further challenges. By working on an unstable base, the Swiss Ball, the body's inner core has no choice but to react!

History of Pilates

The Pilates method was invented during the First World War by German-born Joseph Pilates. While interned in England, he developed the method to assist war veterans and amputees, enabling them to exercise while in their hospital beds. After the war, Joseph set up a studio with his wife Clara in New York and began to train others in his technique. However, Joseph Pilates failed to set up an official training program during his lifetime and this has led to variations in the methods that are taught today. His technique has been adapted to accommodate the more advanced knowledge that we now have about the body, but the essence remains the same: a holistic mind–body approach to fitness. Nowadays, Pilates is used by physical therapists and chiropractors for rehabilitation, by athletes and dancers, and by those who want to get fit.

History of the Swiss Ball

The first Swiss Ball was made by an Italian toymaker, Aquilino Cosani, in the 1960s. Initially it was used in Europe as a tool by physical therapists treating neuromuscular disorders such as MS, cerebral palsy, and spinal injuries. Since then, having seen the huge benefits of working with the ball, athletic coaches and personal trainers have adopted the method for general fitness.

The benefits of Pilates on the ball

Pilates on the ball is quite different from other exercise systems and requires you to tap into a way of working your body that may feel unlike any workout you've tried before. It is not a "quick fix" and can take time to master, with frustrations along the way. It usually takes at least three or four sessions to begin to understand what you are trying to do, but if you stay with it the rewards will be huge. This multidimensional workout is guaranteed to flatten and tone the abdominals, develop longer, leaner muscles, and help improve posture, as well as giving you a true sense of well-being.

The workout focuses on working your body as a whole so that it learns to function as an integrated unit. During movement, the human brain does not think in terms of individual muscles. Instead, it uses them in groups with specifically programed sequences. Often these sequences can be disrupted by injury or bad posture, resulting in poor movement control. Pilates will help to address any imbalances by encouraging the correct sequences, so that the body starts to move with increased ease and efficiency.

Pilates on the ball also challenges your proprioceptors—these provide the body with feedback concerning movement, and create an awareness of a body part or limb. Pilates on the ball can therefore improve your balance, reaction time, and motor (movement) skills, helping to develop muscles that respond quickly and effectively to the challenges we face in everyday life.

Other than the physical benefits, Pilates on the ball is great for relaxation and stress relief. The internal focus can help to calm the mind and the body. Even the simple act of sitting and bouncing up and down on the ball can aid relaxation—smiling or laughing simply cannot be avoided, and it is a great way to release stress and tension.

How to use this book

This book is a great introduction to a Pilates on the ball workout. However, it is not intended as a substitute for a class or a session with a specialized trainer. Before attempting a workout, read through the introductory chapter and the basic principles (chapter 2). Practice the basic principles and build up your confidence on the ball before starting to work through the warm-up and workouts. A full understanding of the basic principles is essential before you start. Once you feel ready to move on, always ensure that you warm up properly and follow the "how to put it together" charts so that you have a balanced workout. You may find it helpful to ask a friend or family member to read out the exercises to you when you first start so that you can focus on the exercise itself.

Getting Started
Equipment
You will need:

- A small cushion (this is used to bring the head and neck into alignment when lying on your back; try a few different sizes until you find one that is comfortable and leaves the back of the neck feeling long)
- A yoga mat (or a clear area of carpet)
- A Swiss Ball

Choosing a ball

Swiss Balls can be bought from most fitness stores and are not expensive. Buy a ball that is burst-resistant so that if it punctures, it will deflate slowly rather than with a bang. Most importantly, the ball should be the correct size in relation to your height. It is recommended that when sitting on the ball the knees should be even with or slightly below the hips, and bent at 90 degrees.

A general guide when choosing a ball:

Your height	Ball diameter
Under 5' 3" (1.6 m)	17" (45 cm)
5' 3" (1.6 m)–5' 8" (1.72 m)	21" (55 cm)
5' 9" (1.75 m)–6' 3" (1.9 m)	25" (65 cm)
6' 4" (1.93 m)–6' 9" (2 m)	29" (75 cm)

Always read the manufacturer's guidelines regarding inflation of the ball. As a rough guide it should be inflated so that it gives slightly when pressed. Remember that the harder the ball the more challenging the exercise will be, so once more strength is achieved, the challenge can be increased by adding more air to the ball.

Environment

Try to find a quiet, comfortable space to work out in (see relaxation section, page 21). Always exercise on a nonslip surface, for example, a yoga mat or clear area of carpet. Ensure the surrounding area is clear so that you can get off without treading on any objects. Also, check the floor for any sharp objects that could puncture the ball.

What to wear

Choose clothes that are comfortable to move in, avoiding baggy clothes as they can get caught under the ball—a T-shirt and shorts or tracksuit pants are ideal. Remove any jewelry and belts with buckles. It is best to avoid working out in socks because these can slip on the ball—bare feet are more suitable.

When, what, and how long?

A Pilates on the ball workout can be undertaken at any time of day. Try to choose a time that fits in easily with your lifestyle and when you feel relaxed and ready to focus. If you suffer from stiffness in the back, choose a time when you feel more mobile, for example at the end of the day or after a walk.

You are more likely to succeed with making this a part of your life if you take time to think about when you can realistically fit a workout into your schedule. Once you have recognized a time that suits you, block out an appointment with yourself in your diary, as you would a meeting at work or a doctor's appointment.

Aim to work out three times a week for between half an hour and an hour. Practice at the essential level 1 three times a week for at least 8–10 weeks before moving on to level 2. Do not rush to move through the levels. Pilates should be learned slowly and with focus. Remember, it's a stroll not a sprint!

Listen to your body. If you feel any muscle soreness the day after your workout, it is recommended that you rest or vary your workout by participating in some cardiovascular work instead, for example, walking, swimming, or cycling.

Precautions
• Drink plenty of water during your workout to prevent muscle soreness and dehydration.
• Don't eat a big meal before exercising—wait at least an hour to aid digestion.
• Do not exercise if you are feeling unwell.

Getting on and off the ball safely

The ball will move and may roll away when you try to get on it. Practice these methods of getting on and off safely a few times before starting your workout.

Supine Incline

1 Start position: Seated on the ball, arms long at the side.

2 To get on: Slowly walk the feet away, walking the spine down the ball so that the lower back comes to rest on the side edge of the ball. Pull the abdominals in and also use the leg and buttock muscles as support.

3 To get off: Push through the feet, walking them in, and move the spine back up the ball, until you are once again in a seated position on top of the ball.

Supine Bridge

Start position: Seated on the ball, arms long at the side.

1 To get on: Slowly walk the feet away so that the spine moves down the ball. Begin to squeeze the buttocks and lift the hips so that you come to a straight line through the knees, hips, and shoulders. Pull the abdominals in to support the back. The upper back and head should be resting comfortably on the top of the ball. The back of the neck should feel long with the eye line to the ceiling.

2 To get off: Tuck the chin into the chest and begin to push through the feet, using the legs to bring yourself back to a seated position on the ball. Work through the spine as above.

Prone

1 **Start position:** Squat in front of the ball with the arms resting on the sides of it.

2 **To get on:** Gently rock forward so that the stomach comes onto the ball and the arms reach the floor. Walk the hands out so that you come to balance on the thighs or the shins (walking further out will make it harder to balance). Pull the abdominals in to support the back.

3 **To get off:** Walk the hands back until the feet and then knees come to the floor and the stomach is back on the ball.

chapter one
the mind–body connection

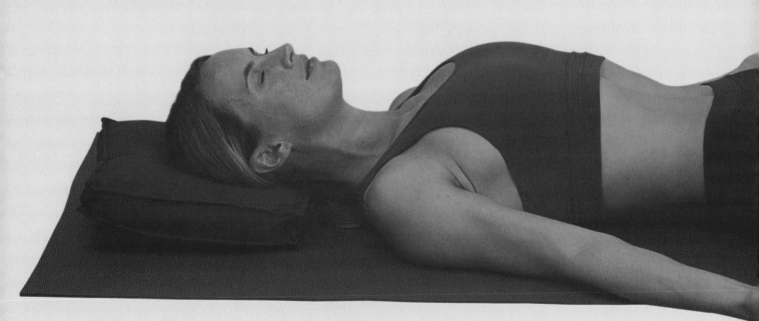

A mind–body connection is the special ingredient in a Pilates on the ball workout. This is the ability to connect the mind to the movements of the body, and to use this connection to move our bodies with precision and control. This chapter is an introduction to the mechanics of the body—bones, muscles, and movements that are needed during the workout. It looks at ideal posture, and explains how to correct bad posture through exercise. The mind focus is also introduced, including the importance of relaxation, with an emphasis on visualization.

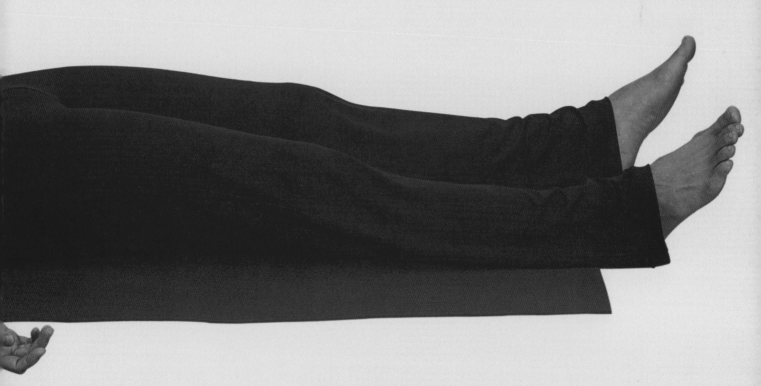

the body

There are 206 bones that link together to form the human skeleton. Pound for pound, bone is as strong as steel, and three times stronger than the same quantity of reinforced concrete! For the purpose of this book we will be most interested in the spine, the pelvis, and the shoulder blades.

Of the 206 bones of the skeleton, 33—called vertebrae —make up the S-shaped curve of the spine. The vertebrae are stacked on top of one another, smaller at the top and larger at the base, with a spongy, shock-absorbent disk between each one. The vertebrae provide an attachment for muscles and also protect the spinal cord, which carries messages from the brain to the muscles via spinal nerves, and from the muscles to the brain. As a result of bad posture or incorrect body use— for example, sitting at a computer for long periods of time—the spine can be drawn out of its natural alignment. Pilates aims to realign bone over bone, to bring the spine back to its natural, most efficient state. There are five segments of the spine:

Cervical: The neck (7 vertebrae).

Thoracic: The upper and midback. This has a slight outward curve and provides an attachment for the rib cage (12 vertebrae).

Lumbar: The lower back with a slight inward curve (5 vertebrae).

Sacrum: These vertebrae are fused and make up part of the pelvis (5 vertebrae).

Coccyx: These vertebrae are fused and are referred to as the tailbone (4 vertebrae).

The pelvis, shaped like a basin, is the central part of the skeleton and is a key focus in Pilates. Imagine that it is an anchor, with the vertebrae of the spine as the movable rope floating vertically upward. The four cornerstones of the pelvis will be referred to later. These are the coccyx, the pubic bone, and the two sit bones. (To feel the sit bones, rock from side to side when seated on a chair; they are just under the crease of the buttocks and you should feel them on the chair as you rock.) The hip bones at the front of the pelvis will also be used as a landmark to help with pelvic placement; these are the most protruding bones at the front of the pelvis, located slightly in from the edge of the hips.

The shoulder blades or scapulae, found in the upper back, are also important. They glide across the surface of the thoracic spine and play an important role in the stabilization and posture of the upper back.

Joints and movements

A joint is where bone and bone meet and where movement occurs. Joints are aligned by ligaments, which connect bone to bone. Overlying the ligaments are muscles that provide the stability of the joint but also create its movement. The four movements of the spine upon which we will focus are extension, flexion, rotation, and lateral flexion.

Extension: The straightening or opening of a joint—for example, to kick a football requires extension of the knee.

Flexion: The bending of a joint or bringing the bones closer together—for example, to bring an apple to the mouth flexes the elbow.

Rotation: A turning movement—for example, to look over your shoulder to check if a car is coming is rotation of the neck and spine.

Lateral flexion: A sideways bend—for example, if you were weighed down by a heavy bag in one hand.

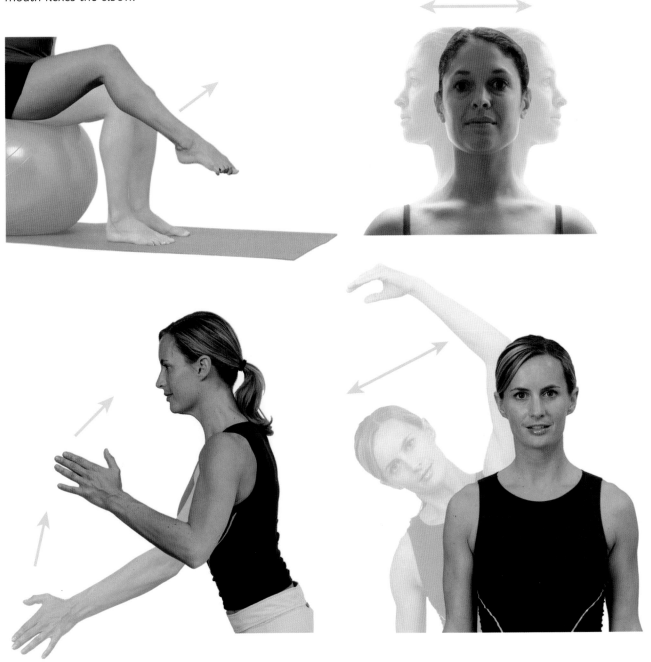

muscles

Muscles are made up of muscle fibers that contract and relax to produce movement. Each muscle fiber is thinner than a human hair but can support up to one thousand times its own weight. Muscles work in pairs: as one contracts, the opposite muscle lengthens—for example, the biceps at the front of the upper arm and the triceps at the back. Tendons and ligaments attach muscles to bones. Each muscle has an origin and insertion that dictates its action.

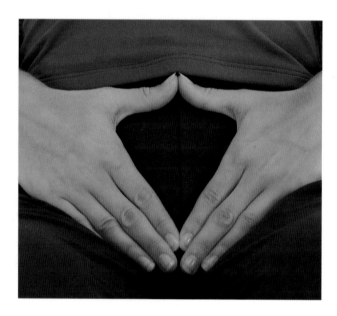

The multifidus supports the spine from the back. This is a group of surprisingly thick, deep muscles that run from vertebra to vertebra down the spine.

The pelvic floor provides the support from below, attaching from the four cornerstones of the pelvis (see page 14). Imagine the pelvic floor as an elastic net, stretched between the bones at the base of the pelvis. Think about drawing the four points of this diamond shape together and up internally toward the belly button. Despite the myth, both women and men have a pelvic floor! Keeping it strong is vital for postural alignment and other issues—for example, continence.

The core muscles

The pelvic floor at the bottom of the pelvis, the multifidus to the back of the spine, and the transverse abdominus at the front make up the inner unit.

The transverse abdominus (TA) is the deepest layer of the abdominals, closest to the spine. These muscles attach from the rib cage down to the pubic bone and around into the back of the body like a corset around the spine. Place your hands on your belly and cough. You will feel the TA push up against your hands.

Abdominal muscles

The three other abdominal muscles are the rectus abdominus, the outer layer (the "six pack"), and the internal and external obliques. The internal and external obliques are the muscles around the side of the torso. They laterally flex (bend to the side) the spine and rotate it. When rotating, the right external oblique works with the left internal to rotate you to the left (and vice versa) and during this movement they can be visualized as a diagonal line across the midsection.

Upper back muscles

The latissimus dorsi ("lats") and trapezius muscles work to stabilize the upper back and shoulder (the lats also stabilize the pelvis). The lats are the broadest muscles in the back (one on each side of the body). They run from the top of the upper arm down to the top of the pelvis, and across into the spine. The action of pulling a window shut uses this muscle. The trapezius is a diamond-shaped muscle running from the base of the skull out to the shoulders and down to a point in the midback. To help release tension in the neck and shoulders, we will be focusing on strengthening the middle and lower fibers of the trapezius (which work to bring the shoulder blades down the back, away from the ears), and releasing the upper fibers either side of the neck.

Hip muscles

The hip muscles have a role to play in postural alignment, too. The hip flexors are the muscles that cross the front of the hip. To lift your knee is a contraction of the hip flexor. The glutei (the buttocks) are a group of muscles that extend the hip. They contract when standing from a seated position.

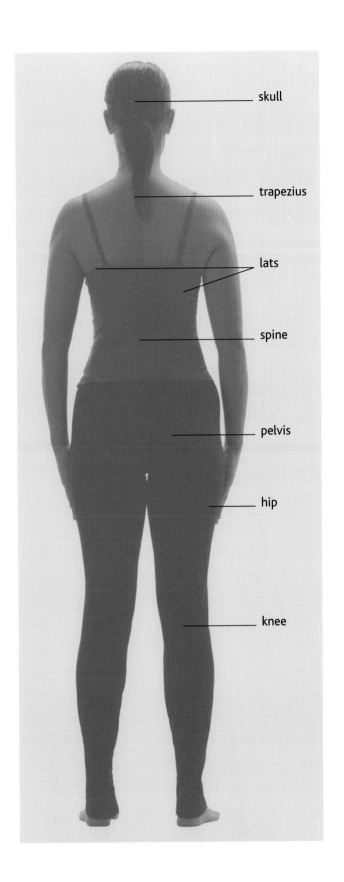

skull

trapezius

lats

spine

pelvis

hip

knee

posture

Posture is the way we sit, stand, and move. Think again about the skeleton and the ideal alignment of its S-shaped curve. When we have good posture, the body is well balanced and we can move without placing the body under unnecessary strain. Those with good posture look taller, slimmer, and more fluid in their movement. However, very few people have perfect posture in adult life. Time spent sitting hunched at a desk, long periods of time standing, or simply favoring one side when carrying can lead to poor posture. This puts our bodies under stress, movement becomes less efficient, and aches or pains can develop.

As well as the external signs of bad posture (for example, rounded shoulders), our internal organs can also suffer and may be pushed out of place, resulting in problems with digestion and respiration. It can take time to correct bad posture. Think of the time it has taken to develop it! Years of standing in a certain way cannot be changed in an instant. However, through Pilates you can start down the road to correction and better posture.

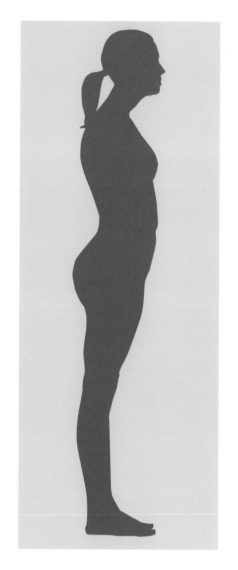

Self-analysis

It is useful to be aware of your postural issues before you start so that you know what you should be focusing on in your workout. Either ask a friend to help or take a picture of yourself, from both the side and the front, and have an honest look at what you can see. Make sure that you are standing as you would naturally; try not to correct your posture by holding your tummy in or your shoulders back.

One common example of poor posture is kyphosis lordosis. This is where the shoulders are rounded and hunched with forward head placement and an increased inward curve in the lower back, resulting in an anterior (forward) tilt of the pelvis. In this posture the upper back muscles (lats and trapezius) and the abdominal muscles may be weak. The chest, hip flexors, and lower back muscles may be tight. Once the muscle imbalances have been identified, we can work correcting them; for example, with a kyphosis lordosis posture, one focus would be to strengthen the abdominals and lengthen the lower back to bring the posture back to the ideal.

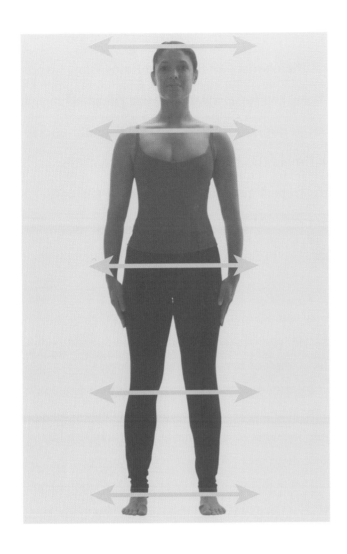

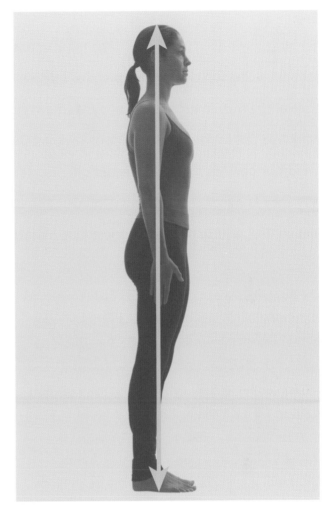

Front view

- Head straight

- Shoulders level with an equal distance between the ears and shoulders

- Rib cage straight with an equal distance between the arms and the body

- Hip bones level

- Knee caps level

- Feet parallel, with the ankle bones level

Side view

Draw a line on your photo from slightly forward of the ankle bone up. Ideally this line will run through:

- Middle of the knee

- Middle of the hip

- Middle of the trunk

- Middle of the shoulder

- Middle of the ear

the mind

The mind connection is the element that differentiates Pilates from other exercise systems. Pilates practice requires us to bring the focus inward; to use the mind to control the movements of the body. We have the power in our minds to change the way our bodies work. We can make muscles relax or contract just by a simple thought. Without this use of the mind, our bodies will merely recruit old muscle patterns to perform the exercises, using the only way they know to create movement. Our aim is to train our bodies to work correctly with precision and control, and to do this we must first train the mind.

The main tool used to gain the mind–body connection is visualization, i.e. imagining a similar or linked image to the required movement or muscle. Throughout the exercise chapters, visualization cues will be used. These will encourage the body to understand the movement required. Try the following exercise:

Close your eyes and bring the focus inward. Imagine that you are standing underneath a waterfall. Feel the water flow over your neck, shoulders, and back. As it flows over you, all the tension in those areas is washed away with it. Now become aware of how the tension through your neck and shoulders has released through this connection between mind and body.

Try also to visualize the muscle that should contract —for example, think about pulling your belly in away from the waist of your pants or sliding your shoulder blade down your back. Don't worry if you find this difficult at first—with a little practice and training you will soon be making swift progress with the way you use your body.

relaxation

It is much easier to tune in to the mind–body focus when you begin your workout in a relaxed state of mind. Before you begin, turn the phone off, send family members out of the room, and shut the door. It may be an idea to put some relaxation music on to help prevent your mind from wandering.

Lie down on your back, with your legs either bent or straight (whatever is most comfortable), and place a small cushion underneath your head. Place your hands at your sides with the palms facing up to the ceiling. Begin to focus on your breathing. Breathe deeply into the body, through the chest, rib cage, and down into the abdomen. Inhale through the nose and exhale through the mouth (breathe out through a straw if this helps). As you breathe, allow your body to relax and any tension to release into the floor. We are going to focus on deepening the breath further.

- Inhale for 4 counts, exhale for 4 counts. Repeat 6 times.
- Inhale for 4 counts, exhale for 6 counts. Repeat 6 times.
- Inhale for 4 counts, exhale for 8 counts. Repeat 6 times.
- Inhale for 4 counts, hold for 2 counts, exhale for 8 counts, hold for 2 counts.

Continue to breathe at this pace for 5–10 minutes. If your mind wanders, bring the focus back to the breath. People have different responses to relaxation. If the above doesn't feel right, try visualizing a beautiful place, somewhere you feel safe and relaxed. Imagine yourself there and breathe slowly and rhythmically.

chapter two

the basic principles

The basic principles of Pilates—breathing and the placement of the pelvis, rib cage, shoulders, head, and neck—will help you to understand how good alignment creates correct movement. It is vital that you understand them properly before you start your workout. This will ensure that each exercise is performed with the required focus, precision, and control, and will enable you to gain the full benefit of each one. The five principles should not be viewed as separate concepts. Instead, they work together to help achieve body control. They also provide us with a checklist for the alignment of the body in every exercise.

This chapter introduces the five basic principles, with exercises to demonstrate each one. Take time to practice these a few times, until you feel confident with all five, before moving on to the warm-up and workouts.

breathing

Breathing is something we do unconsciously all day, every day. However, largely owing to high stress and tension levels, many people breathe shallowly in the upper chest, rather than taking a full deep breath into the lungs. Do you often feel the need to stop and take a deep breath? Do you sigh a lot? If the answer is yes, this could be a sign that you are not breathing properly.

Breathing properly encourages effective oxygenation of the blood (allowing muscles and organs to work efficiently), relaxes muscles, and releases tension. For a Pilates workout, it also helps with the mind–body focus and, importantly, with the contraction of the inner unit.

Pilates breathing is called thoracic or lateral breathing. This means breathing into the side of the body, the thoracic part of the spine, i.e. breathing into the back and sides of the rib cage. The reasons for this are threefold. Firstly, the exchange of gases is most efficient in the lower portion of the lungs. Secondly, breathing wide into the rib cage allows us to relax the neck, chest, and shoulders, reducing tension. Thirdly, the emphasis on breathing into the rib cage leaves the abdominal area free for contraction. With the inhale

through the rib cage rather than into the belly, the breathing pattern allows us to maintain a contraction of the TA (transverse abdominus) on the inhale as well as the exhale, meaning that the stability in the pelvis can be maintained.

The focus is on breathing in through the nose, as this helps to regulate the breath, and out through the mouth, through slightly pursed lips, as if blowing out through a straw, or blowing out a candle. The active exhalation through the mouth encourages a stronger contraction of the pelvic floor and TA, which in turn forces the breath up and out of the lungs. Imagine a tube of toothpaste being squeezed from the bottom—this represents the core muscles pulling in. As the tube is squeezed, the toothpaste—representing the breath—is forced out.

Each exercise has a set breathing pattern, and each movement is linked to a specific breath. Generally, you will breathe in to prepare or hold, and exhale during the movement. This will give you more control during the exercise. Try to follow the breathing patterns closely. Should you run out of air, take another breath in, and then continue the movement on the exhalation. As you continue to practice, you will find it easier to complete the movements on one breath.

Try the following exercise to practice the breathing technique:

1 Start position: Rest the torso over the ball with the head turned to one side, the knees and feet on the floor, arms hugging the ball.

Begin to breathe into the back and side of the rib cage, as though through the gills of a fish. Inhale through the nose and exhale through the mouth, breathing as deeply as you comfortably can. Resist any temptation to hold your breath. Ensure the collarbone (clavicle), shoulders, and neck stay relaxed.

2 Inhale: Rock forward over the ball so that the legs straighten and the hands come to the floor in front of the ball.

Exhale: Roll back so the weight comes into the feet.

Repeat 8–10 times.

Be aware of "over"-breathing. The breath should be gentle and soft. Exaggerated breathing can lead to a tendency to hold the breath, and therefore increase tension.

1

2

pelvic placement

There are two positions for the pelvis—neutral and imprint.

Neutral

Neutral is where the pelvis lies with the natural curve in the lower back, where the spine is most stable and the hip bones and pubic bone are level.

Supine (on your back)

1 Start position: Supine with the legs bent, feet placed hip-distance apart. (You can place a cushion or towel underneath your head to create length in the back of the neck.) Place the palms of the hands onto the hip bones and point the fingers to the pubic bone. The thumbs will come together. The hands will now be lying in a triangle on the abdominals. They represent the position of the pelvis.

2 Inhale: Tilt the pelvis so that the pubic bone and fingers point down toward the mat. Take care not to arch into the rib cage and only go as far as feels comfortable.

3 Exhale: Roll through and draw the lower back toward the mat so that the pubic bone and fingers go up toward the ceiling. Make sure that you don't lift your bottom away from the mat and only go as far as is comfortable.

4

4 Repeat this movement a few times and then settle at the point that feels like halfway. Alternatively, reduce the range of the tilt gradually until you find halfway.

This midway point is your neutral position. The hip bones and pubic bone should be level in neutral. Make sure that you feel comfortable here; that there is no tension in the glutei (the buttocks), the hip flexors (the front of the hips), or in the lower back. If there is, let it go—you may find that the position changes slightly. Once in neutral, become aware of the curve through the lower back, and the distance between the lower back and the floor. Take time to repeat this exercise until you feel confident about how to find it.

Now that neutral has been located, the focus comes to stabilizing it using the core muscles: TA, pelvic floor, and multifidus (see chapter 1).

Stabilizing neutral

The TA (transverse abdominus)

Inhale: Prepare.

Exhale: Draw the TA inward, pulling the belly gently away from the hands. Imagine that there is a rope between your hip bones and think about gently tightening the rope. Alternatively, think about pulling your belly in away from the waistband of your pants. The pelvis should stay still. This contraction should be just 30 percent of the maximum contraction of this muscle. To find 30 percent, firstly pull in as hard as you can, then reduce by half, and then by half again. This may feel very gentle, maybe too gentle, but remember we are working stabilizing muscles. Their job is endurance so they only need to contract to this degree.

Repeat 10 times.

The pelvic floor

Inhale: Prepare.

Exhale: Imagine the pelvic floor attached to the four cornerstones at the bottom of the pelvis: the coccyx, sit bones, and pubic bone. These bones form a diamond shape. Draw the diamond shape together and then up toward the belly button. Think of drawing up internally, as if you were going to the rest room and wanted to stop the flow. The glutei (buttocks) should stay relaxed, so think about engaging the muscle from the front rather than from the back. The pelvis should stay still.

TA and pelvic floor together

Inhale: Prepare.

Exhale: Draw up internally with the pelvic floor and then pull the TA in flat and wide, as if drawing the hip bones away from each other. The pelvis should stay still.

You will focus on the contraction of your core muscles in every exercise you work through. Now try to find neutral in the following positions:

1 Seated on the ball: Repeat as above, rolling through the pelvic range, and finding halfway. You should feel the sit bones on the ball and the hip bones and pubic bone should be level in a vertical position.

2 Exhale: Focus on engaging the pelvic floor and TA. The pelvis stays still.

3 All fours: Repeat as above, rolling through the pelvic range and settling in halfway. The sacrum (lower part of the spine) should be flat, the sit bones pointing out to the wall behind.

4 Exhale: Focus on engaging the pelvic floor and TA. The pelvis stays still.

5 Prone: Roll over the ball (see page 11 for how to get on safely). To stabilize the pelvis here, think about drawing the tailbone (coccyx) toward the heels. Take care not to arch through the back. You will need to use the buttocks and leg muscles as well as your core.

Imprint

Imprint is a slight upward tilt of the pelvis, a lengthening of the lumbar spine, so that the pubic bone is slightly higher than the hip bones, and the lower back is slightly closer to the mat when lying supine. It is attained by engaging the oblique muscles and rectus abdominus, as well as the TA and pelvic floor, to shorten the distance between the hip bones and the rib cage.

Imprint and release

1 Start position: Supine incline on the ball, neutral pelvis, feet placed hip-distance apart directly below the knees, arms long at the side.

Inhale: Prepare.

2 Exhale: Contract the obliques and rectus abdominus to bring the rib cage and hip bones closer toward each other (the pelvic floor and TA should also engage). Feel the spine move into the ball. Take care not to engage the glutei (the buttocks). Make sure that the abdominals stay flat and wide; they should not "dome" or push forward.

Inhale: Release.

Repeat 5 times.

rib cage placement

The abdominals attach to the bottom of the rib cage. Their engagement from this point is important because they work to keep the rib cage in its correct alignment. The focus is on keeping the rib cage flat, avoiding any lifting or "popping" of the rib cage when lying supine, or any forward shift of the pelvis when seated. The movement of the rib cage works with the breath: opening on the inhale and gently closing on the exhale.

Arm Lifts

1 Start position: Seated on the ball with the pelvis in neutral, feet placed hip-distance apart, arms long at the side.

2 Inhale: Reach the arms forward so that they come level with the shoulders.

3 Exhale: Begin to reach the arms toward the ceiling, only going as far as you can without allowing the rib cage to shift forward or "pop" open.

4 Contract your core muscles to stabilize the pelvis in neutral and focus on the feeling of the rib cage sliding down and gently together.

Inhale: Lower the arms down so that they are level with the shoulders.

Exhale: Return to start position.

cervical/head and neck placement

Awareness here is centered on keeping the natural curve of the cervical spine (the neck), with the head balancing on the top. There is a focus on keeping length through the back of the neck, rather than, for example, allowing the chin to reach forward.

In Pilates exercises, the head and neck should generally follow the line of the thoracic spine. When flexing the spine from the floor, the focus needs to be on lengthening the cervical spine into flexion rather than overflexing and jamming the chin to the chest. There should be a small gap between the chin and the chest, as if you are holding an egg there.

Head Nods

1 Start position: Supine, neutral pelvis with the legs resting over the ball (optional cushion underneath the head), arms long at the side.

2 Inhale: Imagine someone is holding your head and gently draws the head away, lengthening the back of the neck, so that the chin comes slightly into the chest. This movement is coming from the top two vertebrae in the neck rather than all seven. It's a small movement; take care not to jam the chin down. The eye line will drop to the knees.

Exhale: Release to neutral; the eye line returns to the ceiling.

You may feel more comfortable with a small cushion underneath your head to help maintain length in the back of the neck.

scapulae/shoulder stability

Shoulder stability is as important as the abdominal contraction. Many people suffer from tension in the neck and shoulders, leading to postural problems and headaches. This is largely due to overworked muscles in the neck and upper back (upper trapezius) and poor use of the stabilizing muscles in the midback. The shoulder stabilizers are a group of muscles in the midback area: serratus anterior, rhomboids, the lats, and lower/midtrapezius (the latter two were described on page 17 in chapter 1). By focusing on a proper use of these muscles, any tension in the neck and shoulders can be greatly reduced.

Scapulae Isolations
(exercises for protraction and retraction)

1 Start position: Seated on a mat, neutral pelvis, holding the ball at shoulder height in front of the body.

2 Inhale: Reach the ball forward, feeling the shoulder blades open (protraction).

Exhale: Release back to neutral.

Repeat 4 times.

3 Inhale: Squeeze the shoulder blades back toward each other (retraction).

Exhale: Release to neutral (shoulder blades should be wide on the back).

Repeat 4 times.

To keep the sense of width across the chest and back, the focus is on settling in a neutral position between the two movements above.

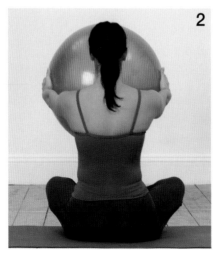
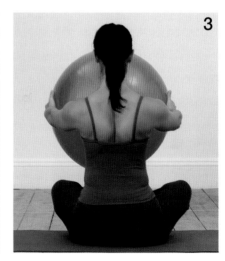

The shoulder blade has no bony attachment so is very mobile. It can rotate, move up, down, inward, and outward. It needs to be able to move with the arm, so needs to be stable without being fixed. The shoulder blade should lie flat on the back of the rib cage without pointing out or rounding forward. The focus is on keeping a sense of width across the chest and back, and a sense of length from the ear down to the shoulder, evenly on both sides.

Elevation and Depression of the Shoulder

1 Start position: Seated on a mat, neutral pelvis, holding the ball to the ceiling.

2 Inhale: Reach the ball to the ceiling; keep the muscles to the side of the neck relaxed.

3 Exhale: Slide the shoulder blades down and slightly together in a V-shape movement toward the pelvis. Focus on the contraction of the shoulder stabilizers. Keep a sense of openness across the chest and back.

The focus is on keeping distance between the ear and the shoulder, along with a feeling of width across the chest and back.

If you feel uncomfortable in your back or hips when seated, try sitting on a small cushion.

chapter three

warm-up

It is essential to warm up the body before starting a Pilates on the ball workout. The warm-up prepares the body, both mentally and physically, for the exercises to follow, and also helps prevent injury. The physical element is mobilizing the spine, pelvis, and other joints. The mental element relates to the mind–body connection already discussed in chapter 1. The warm-up prepares the mind for what's to come, enabling us to focus on the task ahead with more ease. The warm-up also serves to stimulate the pathways from the brain to the body so that the signals between the two become clearer. It demonstrates how to put the basic principles into practice; in fact, the exercises in chapter 2 will be used as part of the warm-up.

This chapter works through the Pilates on the ball warm-up. If you are new to exercise, you may want to start with just the warm-ups for a few weeks before moving on to the essential exercises.

hip release

Focus: Hip mobility.

1 Start position: Supine on the mat with the soles of the feet on the ball, neutral pelvis, arms long at the side.

2 Inhale: Allow both knees to drop open to the side and straighten the legs. The ball will roll away. Keep the hips relaxed and the pelvis neutral. Imagine a bowl of water across the hips and try to keep the water very still in the bowl. Use the core muscles to keep the pelvis steady.

3 Exhale: Roll the legs to parallel and use the legs to draw the ball back in.

Repeat 3–5 times.

Remember to focus on engaging your core muscles to keep the pelvis level.

spinal rotation

Focus: Mobility of the spine in rotation.

1 Start position: Supine on the mat, with the legs resting over the ball, neutral pelvis, arms long at the side.

Inhale: Prepare.

2 Exhale: Engage the core muscles and allow the legs to roll the ball over to one side. Make sure the opposite shoulder stays in touch with the mat and that the rib cage stays connected; avoid arching in the midback.

Inhale: Hold the position as you inhale.

3 Exhale: Engage the abdominals and draw the ball back to the center. Repeat the exercise, this time rolling the ball to the other side.

Repeat 3–5 times each way.

Avoid popping or lifting the rib cage.

Keep a connection in your core on the inhale as well as the exhale.

hip roll

Focus: Mobility of the spine.

1 Start position: Supine with the soles of the feet resting on the ball. Feet placed hip-distance apart, arms long at the side.

Inhale: Prepare.

2 Exhale: Begin by connecting the abdominals to imprint the spine. Continue to roll through, peeling the spine away from the mat one vertebra at a time. Push the feet into the ball. Keep the weight in the upper back and avoid going too high up onto the neck; you should be able to lift your head away from the floor. There should be a straight line through the knees, hips, and shoulders. Use the leg muscles and buttocks to keep the hips lifted and to prevent the ball from rolling away. Think about drawing the tailbone to the back of the knees.

Inhale: Hold the position as you inhale.

3 Exhale: Roll down slowly through the spine, one vertebra at a time, allowing the chest and rib cage to soften. Imagine placing a string of pearls onto the mat.

Repeat 3–5 times.

scapulae isolations

Focus: To bring awareness to the movements of the shoulder blade and improve stability.

1 Start position: Supine bridge, neutral pelvis, core muscles engaged. Feet placed hip-distance apart, directly below the knees. Arms to the ceiling, head resting on the ball (if you feel any tension on your neck, move down the ball a little).

Retraction

Inhale: Squeeze the shoulder blades together.

Exhale: Release to neutral.

Repeat 3–5 times.

Protraction

2 Inhale: Reach to the ceiling; feel the shoulder blades open.

Exhale: Release to neutral.

Repeat 3–5 times.

Use your bottom and legs to hold a good bridge position, with the knees, hips, and shoulders level.

arm circles

Focus: Scapulae stability; opening the shoulders.

1 Start position: Supine bridge, neutral pelvis, core muscles engaged. Feet placed hip-distance apart, directly below the knees. Arms at the side (level with the torso), head resting on the ball.

2 Inhale: Reach the arms up and back (be careful that the rib cage doesn't "pop").

3 Exhale: Circle the arms around and back down to your sides. Think about reaching your fingers to your feet to engage the shoulder stabilizers. Keep the elbows soft.

Repeat 3–5 times.

chest opener

Focus: Opening the chest.

1 Start position: Supine bridge, neutral pelvis, core muscles engaged. Feet placed hip-distance apart, directly below the knees. Arms at the side, head resting on the ball.

2 Inhale: Bring the arms across the chest as if you were giving yourself a hug.

3 Exhale: Open the arms wide to the side. Keep the upper body relaxed.

Repeat 3–5 times.

Remember that the exercises in chapter 2 will also form part of the warm-up. Please refer to the workout charts on pages 90–95 as a guide.

chapter four

essential level 1
(beginner) exercises

Once you have mastered the basic principles and completed the warm-up, you are ready to move on to the Level 1 workout. It is recommended that everyone should practice the exercises at this level three times a week, for 8–10 weeks, however fit they may be.

The exercises focus on improving core stability and work around the movements of the spine (see page 15). Use the workout charts as a guide to ensure that you have a balanced workout, but don't feel you must complete a full set right from the start. The specific focus for each exercise is listed; core and shoulder stability is a focus for all.

It is very important that you feel relaxed and comfortable when practicing these exercises; the focus is on releasing tension, not increasing it. If you feel tension in your lower back, check your neutral position. If there is tension in your hips or lower back when seated, try sitting on a cushion or bending your knees. If the neck feels strained, try placing a cushion underneath the head or bring your awareness to the length in the back of the neck.

ab prep (legs over the ball)

Focus: Flexion of the spine.

1

1 Start position: Supine on the mat with legs resting over the ball. Neutral pelvis, arms resting at the side, back of the neck long (optional cushion underneath the head).

Hip-distance equals one fist distance between the heels or in line with the sit bones. Don't place the feet too wide.

2

Inhale: Lengthen the back of the neck; the chin will drop into the chest slightly, as with Head Nods. Don't jam the chin into the chest and overflex the neck.

As well as the core muscles (pelvic floor and TA), you will be using the rectus abdominus (the "six pack") and the obliques (muscles to the side of the torso) to flex the spine.

Avoid coming up too high and letting the abdominals bulge forward; make sure you are in neutral all the way through the exercise, using the TA to keep the abdominals flat. Make sure the buttocks and hip flexors (front of the hip) stay relaxed. If they contract they could affect your neutral position.

2 Exhale: Slide the shoulder blades down toward the pelvis to stabilize the shoulders, as if reaching the fingers to the feet. Engage the abdominals and focus on sliding the rib cage down toward the pelvis as you flex the spine and lift the head and shoulders away from the mat. Lift the arms a little way off the mat so that they are level with the shoulders. Maintain a neutral position in the pelvis—the hip bones and pubic bone should stay level. Keep the shoulders open and the eye line toward the knees; imagine that you are holding an egg between the chin and the chest.

Inhale: Hold the position as you inhale.

3 Exhale: Keep the chin in toward the chest, the eye line forward, and lower the head and shoulders slowly back down to the mat. Make sure the rib cage stays connected and closed as you lower.

Repeat 5–10 times.

3

breaststroke level 1

Focus: Extension of the spine.

1 Start position: Kneel with the torso resting over the ball, neutral pelvis, hands either side of the ball with the elbows bent.

Inhale: Prepare.

2 Exhale: Engage the core muscles; slide the shoulder blades down and slightly together (in a V-shaped movement toward the base of the spine) as the spine extends, bringing the head and shoulders away from the ball. Allow the head and neck to follow the line of the thoracic spine. Avoid looking too far forward as this will take the neck out of alignment; focus instead on length in the back of the neck.

Inhale: Hold the position as you inhale.

Exhale: Lower to the ball.

Repeat 5–10 times.

Focus on length in the spine, from the top of the head down to the lower back. Make sure the core muscles (pelvic floor and TA) are engaged to support your lower back.

shell

Focus: Release tension.

1 Start position: Kneel, sitting back onto the heels, hugging the ball with the head turned to one side.

Inhale: Prepare.

2 Exhale: Rock forward with the ball and let it come toward the floor. The bottom will lift away from the heels.

Inhale: Return.

Repeat 3–5 times.

Focus on breathing wide into the back and side of the rib cage as you rest over the ball.

the hundred (seated on the ball)

Focus: Abdominal endurance, coordination of the arm movement with the breath, and circulation.

1 Start position: Seated on the ball, neutral pelvis, feet placed hip-distance apart, arms at the side. The breathing pattern for this exercise is a little different as you breathe in for 5 and out for 5 with the movement of the arms. The movement is that of pumping the arms at the side. Think of bouncing a ball with a straight arm.

2 Inhale: For 5 counts, as you pulse the arms gently at your side. Imagine that you are bouncing a ball with each straight arm.

3 Exhale: For 5 counts as you continue to pulse the arms at your side.

Repeat 10 times (this equals 100 breaths).

Think about sitting tall on the ball so that your body stays in alignment as you pulse the arms. Part of the challenge of this exercise is to keep the body still against the movement of the arms. You will need to engage your core muscles (pelvic floor and TA) all the way through to help keep you steady. Think also about the shoulder stabilizers in the upper back.

half roll back

Focus: Flexion of the lower back; movement of the pelvis away from the thigh bone.

1 Start position: Seated on the ball, neutral pelvis, upper body flexed forward with the arms at shoulder height. The head and neck follow the line of the spine so the top of the head lengthens forward; the shoulders are away from the ears. Feet placed hip-distance apart.

Inhale: Prepare.

2 Exhale: Use the abdominals to draw the ball underneath you so that the sacrum (lower part of the spine) rolls back onto the ball. Imagine there is paint on the sacrum, and try to dot the paint onto the ball. The eye line will come to the hands as you roll back. The shoulders stay away from the ears; connect the shoulder stabilizers.

Inhale: Use the abdominals to roll forward to the start position.

Repeat 5–8 times.

Focus on a sense of openness through the front of the hips as you roll back. Also, keep the shape of the spine throughout the movement; it should be in a C-shape.

roll up prep

Focus: Flexion of the spine.

1 Start position: Supine bridge, neutral pelvis, arms reaching out behind but without the rib cage lifting. Feet placed hip-distance apart, directly below the knees.

2 Inhale: Float the arms to the ears and draw the chin to the chest (focus on length in the back of the neck; this movement comes from the top 2 vertebrae, not all 7).

3 Exhale: Engage the abdominals; slide the rib cage to the pelvis as you lift the head and shoulders off the ball. Reach the arms toward the knees. Maintain a straight line from the hips to the knees; use the buttocks and hamstrings to stabilize. The eye line is straight ahead.

Inhale: Maintain the flexion and bring the arms to the ears.

Exhale: Lower the head and shoulders back onto the ball. Keep the connection of the rib cage as you lower.

Repeat 5–8 times.

See the tips in the introduction (page 10) on how to get on and off the ball safely. Supine bridge is a more challenging position for the body as it is less supported by the ball. Make sure you engage the glutei (buttocks) and hamstrings (back of the thighs) to help you maintain a strong bridge position.

spine twist

Focus: Rotation of the spine.

1 Start position: Seated on the ball, neutral pelvis, feet placed on the floor hip-distance apart. Arms placed across the chest.

Inhale: Prepare.

2 Exhale: Engage the core muscles as you rotate the spine. Focus on contracting the oblique muscles to create the movement. Remember that the right external oblique (under the rib cage) and the left internal oblique (above the hip bone) will pull you to the left, and the opposite muscles will pull you to the right. Think about them pulling together in a diagonal line across the torso. Keep the shoulders stabilized and the chin in the middle of the chest. As you rotate, think about lengthening the spine as if it is spiraling as you turn.

Inhale: Return to the center.

Exhale: Repeat other side.

Repeat 3–5 times each way.

> Keep your knees in line; if they move
> it is a sign that your pelvis is not stable.

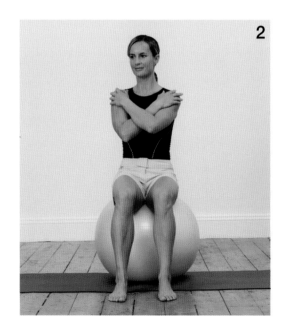

one leg circle

Focus: Mobility of the hip.

1 Start position: Supine; neutral pelvis. One leg bent with the foot on the floor, the other leg in tabletop position, i.e. the leg is lifted so that the knee is in line with the hip and the leg is bent at 90 degrees. Hold the ball in both hands, reaching up to the ceiling but ensuring the shoulders are stabilized (width across the chest and shoulders away from the ears). Imagine that you are going to draw a circle on the ceiling with your knee.

2 Inhale: For the first half of the circle as the leg comes into the midline of the body.

3 Exhale: For the second half of the circle as the leg moves out to the side. Make sure that the pelvis stays steady throughout the circle; the core muscles should be engaged throughout. Imagine that you have a bowl of water across your hip bones and focus on keeping the water level still. Keep the circle as small as is needed to keep the pelvis steady.

Repeat 5 circles in each direction with one leg, then repeat with the other leg.

> Relax the leg that is circling. Imagine that the thigh bone is floating in the hip socket.

single leg stretch

Focus: Stability of the pelvis when working unilaterally (one leg at a time).

1 Start position: Supine; neutral pelvis. Right leg bent with the knee over the hip and the foot resting on the ball, left leg reaching up to the ceiling. Head resting down on the mat, arms long at the side (option of cushion underneath the head).

Inhale: Prepare.

2 Exhale: Engage the core muscles and switch legs. The right leg reaches to the ceiling and the left leg pushes into the ball. Think of pressing into the ball with the left leg (engaging the buttocks and hamstrings), while the toes of the right reach to the ceiling.

Inhale: Begin to switch legs.

3 Exhale: Complete the switch and fully extend the left leg to the ceiling. The right leg is pressing into the ball.

Repeat 8–10 times.

To make this exercise harder, try flexing the upper body away from the mat, as with the Ab Prep. Support your head by placing both hands to the back of the head. Focus on keeping the flexion all the way through the exercise and keep the eye line to the thighs.

roll over prep

Focus: Flexion of the lumbar spine.

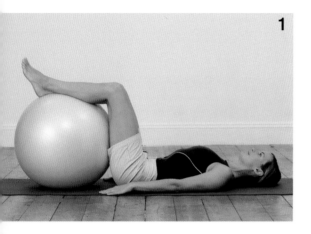

1

2

1 Start position: Supine; neutral pelvis. Both legs bent, resting over the ball. Arms long at the side.

Inhale: Prepare.

2 Exhale: Engage the abdominals to imprint the spine toward the mat and, gripping the ball gently with the legs, roll the ball up, away from the floor. The knees will come closer in toward the chest. Make sure the shoulders stay open and stabilized and the back of the neck stays long. Don't worry about how far the ball is lifting; go as far as feels comfortable. Make sure you are using the abdominal muscles to create the movement and avoid pushing with the arms.

Inhale: Return.

Repeat 6–8 times.

Use the buttocks and the hamstrings (back of the legs) to help lift the ball. Don't "grip" or overuse the hip flexors at the front.

Imprint is the second position used for the pelvis in Pilates, a slight upward tilt, bringing the hip bones and pubic bone closer together. This is initiated by the obliques and rectus abdominus; the buttocks should stay relaxed and the shoulders should stay open. The core muscles should also be engaged.

heel squeeze prone

Focus: Glutei (buttocks) and hamstrings (back of the thighs).

Start position: Prone (on your front); neutral pelvis. Legs hip-distance apart, bent at 90 degrees with the ball between the heels and the back of the thighs. Forehead rests on the hands. Shoulders stabilized.

Inhale: Prepare.

Exhale: Contract the core muscles and push the heels into the ball, engaging the hamstrings and the glutei. Make sure that the hip bones and pubic bone stay in contact with the mat.

Inhale: Release.

Repeat 8–10 times.

To get into position, kneel and place the ball between the heels and the thighs. Gently squeeze the ball and transition down to lying.

single leg extension

Focus: Hip extensors: glutei and hamstrings.

1 Start position: Prone over the ball resting on the thighs; neutral pelvis. Hands below the shoulders, shoulders stabilized. Core muscles engaged.

Inhale: Prepare.

2 Exhale: Engage the glutei and lift one leg off the ball. Don't worry about how high the leg is lifting; focus on maintaining the pelvis and spine in neutral. Use the core muscles and the obliques to prevent the back arching or the pelvis tilting.

Take care getting on and off the ball. First, kneel in front of the ball with the arms resting over it. Then gently rock forward so that the stomach comes onto the ball and the arms reach the floor. Walk the hands out so that you come to balance on the thighs. Pull the abdominals in to support the back. To get off the ball, walk the hands back until the feet and then knees come to the floor.

Inhale: Lower the leg.

Exhale: Lift the other leg.

Repeat 6–8 times on each leg.

scapulae stability (over the ball)

Focus: Scapulae stability.

1 Start position: Prone over the ball resting either on the thighs or shins (the challenge to the core muscles is increased if the body is further forward over the ball). Neutral pelvis, hands below the shoulders, shoulders stabilized. Core muscles engaged. Legs together; engage the buttocks and leg muscles to help maintain the alignment.

2 Inhale: Squeeze the shoulder blades together (retraction). Watch that you don't let the rib cage push forward; use the core muscles and the obliques to keep the spine aligned.

Exhale: Return to neutral placement of the shoulder.

Repeat 4 times.

3 Inhale: Push into the floor so that the shoulder blades open (protraction). Again, focus on the alignment of the spine; it should stay long.

Exhale: Return to neutral placement of the shoulder.

Repeat 4 times.

> Remember to focus on the five basic principles at all times: breathing and the position of the pelvis, rib cage, shoulders, head, and neck.

push-ups (hands on the ball)

Focus: Pectoral muscles (chest) and triceps (back of the arm).

1 Start position: Kneel with the torso resting on the ball. There should be a long line from the head, through the hips and to the knees. Neutral pelvis, shoulders stabilized. Hands placed on the ball.

Inhale: Prepare.

2 Exhale: Push away from the ball so that the arms straighten. Use your core muscles to keep the alignment of the pelvis and spine; do not arch in the lower back.

3 Inhale: Return. Try not to lean on the ball.

Repeat 10 times.

Throughout the exercise, be aware of your shoulder placement; use your shoulder stabilizers (lats and trapezius) to keep the shoulders away from the ears. Also, keep width between the shoulder blades as you return to the ball. They should not "wing" or point out.

mermaid

Focus: Lateral flexion.

1 Start position: Seated on the ball, neutral pelvis, feet on the floor placed hip-distance apart. Arms long at the side.

2 Inhale: Reach one arm up to the ceiling.

3 Exhale: Lean over to the side, reaching the arm over the head. Keep the weight even through the sit bones. Eye line forward.

Inhale: Reach the arm up to the ceiling and bring the body back to a vertical.

Exhale: Lower the arm to the side.

Repeat the exercise, leaning to the other side.

Repeat 3 times on each side.

Try not to lean forward or backward; imagine that you are moving between two sheets of glass.

chapter five

essential level 2 exercises

When you feel confident that you can perform the level 1 exercises with the required control, you are ready to move on to level 2. This chapter shows how to progress some of the level 1 exercises and also introduces some new challenges. A key element with a Pilates on the ball workout is to work with precision and control, using the correct muscles to perform the exercises.

Make sure that you warm up properly before you start, and that you are relaxed and comfortable throughout each exercise. You should aim to practice at level 2 three times a week, for at least 8–10 weeks, before moving on to the intermediate level. Please refer to the workout charts to guide you when putting your workout together. This will ensure a balanced workout including all movements of the spine—flexion, extension, rotation, and lateral flexion.

The focus for each exercise is listed so that you are aware of what you are aiming for—core and shoulder stability is a focus for all. Think of your five basic principles throughout, and try to stay as closely as you can to the breathing pattern as it is detailed.

ab prep (in supine bridge)

Focus: Flexion of the spine.

1 Start position: Supine bridge; neutral pelvis. Engage the core muscles, glutei, and hamstrings to maintain a straight line from the shoulders to the hips and the knees. Feet placed hip-distance apart. Arms long at your sides, palms facing down, shoulders stabilized. Upper back and head resting on the ball.

2 Inhale: Lengthen the back of the neck, bringing the chin into the chest, as with Head Nods. Watch that you don't jam the chin down.

3 Exhale: Engage the abdominals as you flex the spine and lift the head and shoulders away from the ball. Keep the elbows open. Focus on the feeling of drawing the rib cage down to the pelvis. Take care to keep the alignment of the torso in supine bridge; use the glutei and hamstrings to keep the hips lifted.

Inhale: Hold the position as you inhale.

Exhale: Keep the chin tucked into the chest, as if holding an egg, as you lower the head and shoulders back to the ball. Focus on sliding the rib cage to the pelvis as you lower.

Repeat 5–10 times.

As well as the core muscles, you will be using the rectus abdominus (the "six pack") and the obliques to flex the spine.

breaststroke level 2

Focus: Extension of the spine.

1 Start position: Kneel with the torso resting over the ball, neutral pelvis, arms at the side, palms facing in toward the body.

Inhale: Prepare.

2 Exhale: Engage the core muscles, slide the shoulder blades down toward the pelvis (in a V-shape toward the base of the spine) as you extend the spine and lift the head and shoulders away from the ball. Think about drawing the fingers to the knees to help engage the shoulder stabilizers. As you extend the spine, straighten the legs, pushing into the heels. Use your legs and buttocks to extend the legs. The head and neck should follow the line of the thoracic (upper) spine. Imagine drawing the crown of the head to the wall in front of you, and a straight line from the top of your head down to your heels. Keep the eye line down; avoid looking forward as this takes the neck out of alignment.

Inhale: Hold the position as you inhale.

Exhale: Bend the legs, come back onto the knees, and lower the upper body back over the ball.

Repeat 8–10 times.

After the Breaststroke, release with the Shell (see page 47).

Make sure your core muscles are engaged to support your lower back.

the hundred

Focus: Abdominal endurance; coordination of the arm movement with the breath; circulation.

1 Start position: Supine incline (or supine bridge for a harder option), neutral pelvis, feet placed hip-distance apart, arms long at the side. Hip-distance equals one fist distance between the heels or in line with the sit bones. Don't place the feet too wide.

The breathing pattern changes for this exercise, breathing in for 5 and out for 5 to match the movement of the arms. The movement is that of pumping the arms at the side, as if you were bouncing a ball with a straight arm.

2 Inhale: For 5 as you pulse the arms at your side. Use your legs and bottom as support in supine incline. If you are working in supine bridge make sure there is a straight line through your shoulders to the hips and the knees. To help maintain this position, think about drawing the tailbone to the back of the knees; engage the buttocks and hamstrings.

3 Exhale: For 5 as you pulse the arms at your side.

Repeat 10 times (this equals 100 breaths).

Although it's fun to bounce the ball, part of the challenge of this exercise is to keep it steady. Use your core muscles and your shoulder stabilizers for control.

full roll up

Focus: Flexion of the spine.

1 **Start position:** Supine bridge, neutral pelvis. Engage the core muscles, glutei, and hamstrings to maintain a straight line from the shoulders to the hips and the knees. Feet placed hip-distance apart. Arms reaching out behind, without allowing the rib cage to lift.

2 **Inhale:** Bring the arms up to the ceiling and the chin into the chest (focus on length in the back of the neck; this movement comes from the top two vertebrae only).

Exhale: Engage the abdominals as you flex the spine so that the head and shoulders lift from the ball.

3 Now begin to push through the feet, walking them in toward the ball as you continue to flex the spine, working through one vertebra at a time.

4 Roll all the way through the spine until you are seated on the ball. The pelvis is vertical and in neutral, while the spine is flexed forward (as if rounding over a big ball). The arms reach toward the feet. Make sure the shoulder stabilizers are engaged so that the shoulders are away from the ears.

Inhale: Begin to roll back through the spine. Think about drawing the sacrum (lower part of the spine) to the ball as with the Half Roll Back on page 49. Think of rolling through one vertebra at a time.

Exhale: Walk the feet out so that you return to the supine bridge position. Take the arms out behind; watch that the rib cage doesn't "pop".

Repeat 5–8 times.

half roll back with obliques

Focus: Flexion of the lumbar spine with rotation.

1 Start position: Seated on the ball, neutral pelvis. Arms reaching out in front, level with the shoulders. Shoulders stabilized. Feet placed hip-distance apart below the knees.

Inhale: Prepare.

2 Exhale: Use the abdominals to draw the ball under you, bringing the sacrum toward the ball and taking the spine into a C-curve. At the same time rotate the spine to the right, sweeping the right arm down to the floor and then to the wall behind.

Inhale: Maintain the abdominal contraction as you return to face front, sweeping the arm back down to the floor and bringing it in front, level with the shoulders.

Exhale: Repeat on the other side.

Repeat 3–5 times each side.

Focus on shoulder stability and think of length in the back of the neck. Avoid letting the shoulders lift and the chin push forward.

Make sure that the knees stay in line as you rotate; if they move, it is a sign that the pelvis is not stable.

side leg lift

Focus: Hip abduction (leg moves away from the midline).

1

Start position: Side of the torso and hip rest on the ball, neutral pelvis. Kneel on the supporting leg, other leg extended to the side. The body is in a long line. Hands rest on the ball to stabilize.

1 Inhale: Lift the leg up with the foot pointed. Make sure that the hip bones face forward; don't lift the leg too high. Keep both sides of the waist long.

2 Exhale: Lower the leg down with the foot flexed (toes forward).

Repeat 5–10 times, then turn over and repeat with the other leg.

Take care how you get into position. Kneel first and then lean the body onto the ball, using the arms for support.

2

push-ups (over the ball)

Focus: Pectoral muscles (chest) and triceps (back of the arm).

1 Start position: Prone over the ball, neutral pelvis. Rest on either the thighs or shins (the latter is more challenging). Legs together; core muscles, glutei, and leg muscles engaged to maintain alignment in the spine (straight through shoulders, hips, and knees). Hands placed below the shoulders. Shoulders stabilized, back of the neck long.

2 Inhale: Bend the elbows so that the chest comes toward the mat. Do not lead with the chin; instead keep length in the back of the neck. Keep the shoulder blades wide; they shouldn't pinch together as you lower.

Exhale: Push back to a straight line through the shoulders, hips, and knees. Keep the shoulder blades wide; they shouldn't round as you return.

Repeat 10 times.

To get on the ball, kneel in front of it, resting the arms over it. Gently rock forward so that the stomach comes onto the ball and the arms reach the floor. Walk the hands out so that you balance on the thighs or shins. Pull the abdominals in and engage the buttocks to support the back. To get off the ball, walk the hands back until the feet and then knees come to the floor.

Keep the inner thighs together as this will help to connect the pelvic floor.

seated leg lifts

Focus: Stability of the pelvis challenged unilaterally; balance on the ball.

1 Start position: Seated on the ball, neutral pelvis. Feet placed hip-distance apart. Arms out to the sides.

Inhale: Prepare.

2 Exhale: Engage the core muscles and lift one leg away from the floor, keeping the leg bent. Sit tall on the ball and stay even on the sit bones; avoid rounding or arching the lower back as the leg lifts. Keep the hip bones level throughout.

Inhale: Lower the foot back to the floor. Again, focus on preventing any tilt or shift of the pelvis by using the core muscles to stabilize.

Exhale: Repeat with the other leg.

Repeat 5 times on each leg.

2

1

mermaid with rotation

Focus: Lateral flexion.

1

1 Start position: Seated on the ball, neutral pelvis. Feet on the floor placed hip-distance apart. Arms long at the side.

2 Inhale: Reach one arm up to the ceiling.

3 Exhale: Engage the core muscles as you lean over to the left, reaching the right arm over the head. Keep the weight even through the sit bones and the shoulders away from the ears. Eye line forward.

Inhale: Hold the position as you inhale.

4 Exhale: Rotate and look down toward the left leg, reaching the arm out in front of you. Draw the core muscles in to keep the pelvis in neutral and increase the stretch through the spine.

Inhale: Rotate back so that the torso is facing forward, leaning to the side with the arm over the head.

Exhale: Reach the arm up to the ceiling and bring the body back to a vertical position. Lower the arm to the side.

Repeat the exercise on the other side.

Repeat 3 times each side.

2

3

4

chapter six

intermediate exercises

So now the fun really begins! Once you feel confident that you have mastered both the level 1 and level 2 essential exercises, you are ready to move on to the intermediate level. Remember that it is important not to rush or skip the earlier levels. They provide you with the foundation you need to execute the harder exercises with the right focus and control and, importantly, by recruiting the correct muscles. The exercises in this chapter add extra challenge to the core muscles but also challenge the body and mind by increasing coordination. It is vital that you keep your focus on the five basic principles during the exercises and ensure you keep good form throughout. The focus for each exercise is listed so that you are aware of what you are aiming for; core and shoulder stability is a focus for all. Make sure that you warm up properly and follow the workout charts as a guide to how to fit these new exercises into your current workout.

one leg circle (hips lifted)

Focus: Mobility of the hip.

1 Start position: Supine; neutral pelvis. Lower legs resting on the ball, arms long at the side.

Inhale: Prepare.

2 Exhale: First lift the hips away from the mat so that there is a line from the knees, through the hips to the shoulders. You will be resting on your upper back, not on the head and neck. Engage your core muscles and buttocks to support you and think of drawing the tailbone to the back of the knees.

3 Then lift one leg away from the ball and extend it to the ceiling. If it is uncomfortable in the hamstring, just lift it to the tabletop position (knee in line with the hip, leg bent at 90 degrees). Imagine that you are going to draw a circle on the ceiling with the knee.

Inhale: For the first half of the circle as the leg comes into the midline of the body.

4 Exhale: For the second half of the circle as the leg moves out to the side. Make sure that the pelvis stays steady as the leg circles; the core muscles should be engaged throughout. Keep the circle small so that you can keep the hip bones level. You will also need to use the muscles in the supporting leg to hold you steady. Try to keep your shoulders relaxed; use your shoulder stabilizers to avoid tension in the upper back and neck.

Repeat 3 circles in each direction and on each leg.

double leg stretch

Focus: Flexion of the spine; coordination.

1 Start position: Supine; neutral pelvis. Feet resting on the ball with the legs together. Arms long at the side. Back of the neck long (optional cushion or towel underneath the head).

Inhale: Lengthen the back of the neck; the chin comes in toward the chest. Avoid jamming the chin into the chest; keep an egg-sized gap.

2 Exhale: Engage the abdominals as you flex and lift the upper body, as with the Ab Prep (see page 62). Lift the arms away from the mat so that they are level with the shoulders. Eye line is to the thighs.

Inhale: Prepare.

3 Exhale: Reach the arms to the ceiling, bending the elbows on the way as if you are taking a hat off your head. At the same time, extend the legs and roll the ball away from you.

4 Inhale: Circle the arms around and down to your sides. At the same time, bend the legs and use the hamstrings to draw the ball back toward you.

Repeat 5–10 times.

Keep the upper body flexed all the time, with the eye line to the knees. When you circle the arms, keep them within your vision; don't take them out behind you. Watch also that you don't "dome" in the abdominals; keep them flat and wide throughout.

full breaststroke

Focus: Extension of the spine.

1 **Start position:** Prone over the ball with the midsection resting on the ball, neutral pelvis. Legs extended, balls of the feet placed hip-distance apart on the floor. Hands resting on the ball, back of the neck long.

Inhale: Prepare.

2 **Exhale:** Engage your core muscles as you reach the arms forward and round over the ball. Keep a sense of openness across the shoulders and the shoulders away from the ears.

3 **Inhale:** Circle the arms around to the side and back to the ball as you take the spine into extension.

4 Allow the head and neck to follow the line of the spine; avoid looking too far forward and shortening in the back of the neck. Focus on engaging the shoulder stabilizers to bring the shoulder blades toward the pelvis and slightly together in a V-shape toward the base of the spine as you extend.

Repeat 8–10 times.

Release with the Shell (see page 47).

Imagine diving into a pool on the exhale and then pulling the arms back through the water on the inhale.

Use your buttock muscles and hamstrings all the time to keep the alignment of the spine. The core muscles, pelvic floor, and TA should also be engaged throughout.

The shoulder stabilizers are a group of muscles in the upper back, including the lats and lower/midtrapezius. To encourage the engagement of these muscles, think about contracting just underneath the armpit on the back for the lats, and between the shoulder blades for the trapezius.

3

4

leg pull front

Focus: Abdominal endurance, shoulder stability, hip mobility, and strength.

1 Start position: Kneel on all fours with the shins resting against the ball. Neutral pelvis. Hands placed underneath the shoulders, shoulder stabilizers engaged. Back of the neck long, eye line to the floor.

Inhale: Prepare.

2 Exhale: Lift the knees and extend the legs so that the ball moves away. You will end up in a plank position with a straight line through the feet, hips, and shoulders. Think of drawing the tailbone to the feet as you extend the legs to help maintain a neutral position in the pelvis; do not allow the pelvis to tilt or the lower back to arch.

Inhale: Draw the ball back.

Repeat 3–5 times.

Use the muscles in your legs to support you: buttocks, hamstrings, and inner thighs, as well as your core. Make sure that the shoulders are stabilized. Focus on length in the back of the neck; imagine that there is a pole running down your back and focus on keeping the back of your head against the pole.

elephant (round back)

Focus: Flexion of the lumbar spine.

1 Start position: Prone over the ball resting on the thighs. Pelvis in imprint (in a slight upward tilt), spine flexed with the chin toward the chest. Hands placed below the shoulders, shoulder stabilizers engaged. Core muscles and obliques engaged. Legs together; buttocks and leg muscles engaged to help maintain the alignment.

Inhale: Prepare.

2 Exhale: Use the abdominal muscles to draw the ball toward the hands. The bottom will lift to the ceiling. Try not to shift the weight onto the hands as this may unbalance you. Imagine drawing your belly button to the ceiling and think of shortening the distance between the hip bones and rib cage.

Inhale: Allow the ball to move away a little but not all the way to the start position.

Repeat 10 times.

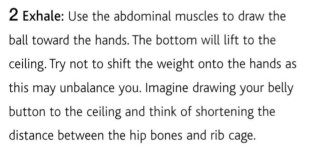

side twist

Focus: Rotation of the spine.

1 Start position: Seated on the ball, neutral pelvis. Feet placed hip-distance apart. Arms reaching out to the side, level with the shoulders, palms down.

Inhale: Prepare.

2 Exhale: Engage the core muscles as you lift the right leg and rotate to the right side. Place the right hand on the ball. Keep your hip bones level as you turn. Focus on contracting the oblique muscles to create the movement. Remember the left external oblique (under the rib cage) and the right internal oblique (above the hip bone) will pull you to the right. Think about them pulling together in a diagonal line across the torso. Keep the shoulders away from the ears and the chin in the middle of the chest.

2

1

3 Inhale: Return to the center. Lower the leg and bring the arm back to shoulder height.

4 Exhale: Lift the left leg as you rotate to the left side. Place the left hand on the ball for support.

Inhale: Return to the center. Lower the leg and bring the arm back to shoulder height.

Repeat 3–5 times each way.

Focus on length through the spine as you turn; imagine that the crown of the head is reaching to the ceiling.

4

3

mermaid with chest opener

Focus: Lateral flexion with chest opener.

1 **Start position:** Seated on the ball, neutral pelvis. Feet on the floor placed hip-distance apart. Arms long at the side.

Inhale: Reach the right arm up to the ceiling.

2 **Exhale:** Engage the core muscles as you lean over to the left, reaching the arm over the head. Keep the weight even through the sit bones and the shoulders away from the ears.

3 **Inhale:** Rotate and look down toward the left leg, reaching the arm out in front.

Remember to focus on the five basic principles at all times: breathing and the position of the pelvis, rib cage, shoulders, head, and neck.

4 Exhale: Rotate back so that the torso is facing forward, leaning to the side with the arm over the head.

5 Inhale: Open the chest and reach behind so that you feel an openness across the chest. The eye line comes to the ceiling.

6 Exhale: Return to the center so that the torso is facing forward, leaning to the side with the arm over head.

Inhale: Reach the arm up to the ceiling.

Exhale: Bring the body back to a vertical position. Lower the arm to the side.

Repeat the exercise on the other side.

Repeat 3 times each side.

chapter seven

stretch and release

The perfect way to end a workout is to stretch and release your muscles and allow your mind to relax after the challenge of the exercises. In this chapter you will be shown stretches for the spine and for the muscles around the hip. Try to hold each stretch for between 30 seconds and one minute. Breathe into the stretch and use your core muscles to support you.

If you have time, a 5- or 10-minute relaxation is a lovely way to finish your workout. Either refer to the relaxation exercise described in chapter one or listen to some calming music while you lie comfortably, focusing on your breath.

cat stretch

Focus: Mobility of the spine.

1 Start position: Kneel as if on all fours but with the hands resting on the ball. Neutral pelvis. Knees placed hip-distance apart. Hands placed shoulder-distance apart.

Inhale: Prepare.

2 Exhale: Engage the abdominals and draw the tailbone to the floor, rolling the ball toward the knees.

3 The spine will come to a vertical position, with the knees, hips, and shoulders in a straight line, the ball resting against the thighs. Keep the chin into the chest so that the neck is slightly flexed forward.

Inhale: Hold the position as you inhale.

Exhale: Lengthen back to the start position, allowing the ball to roll away. Make sure that you maintain a neutral position as you return; avoid going into an anterior (forward) tilt of the pelvis. Use your abdominals to prevent this.

Repeat 3–5 times.

> Keep the shoulders away from the ears;
> apply a light pressure to the ball to help
> engage the shoulder stabilizers.

spine stretch forward

Focus: Mobility of the spine.

1 Start position: Seated on the ball, neutral pelvis. Feet placed hip-distance apart. Hands rest on the side of the ball.

Inhale: Prepare.

Exhale: Engage the core muscles as you lengthen through the back of the neck, dropping the chin into the chest. Begin to roll down through the spine as if you were rolling away from a wall. Think of peeling away one vertebra at a time. Allow the chest to soften and then the rib cage to soften as you roll down.

2 Just go as far as feels comfortable; don't force the stretch. The arms will reach slightly forward of the knees as the spine flexes forward. Relax the shoulders so that they don't lift to the ears. Think of the crown of the head, rather than the chin, coming toward your thighs.

Inhale: Hold the position as you inhale.

Exhale: Begin to lengthen up through the spine, stacking one vertebra on top of the other. Think about creating length between the vertebrae as you return to vertical. Allow the shoulders to drop away from the ears and focus on a feeling of length in the back of the neck.

Repeat 3–5 times.

hip flexor stretch

Focus: Hip flexors (front of the hip).

1 Start position: Seated on the ball, facing the side. One leg bent with the foot on the floor, the other leg bent with the knee toward the floor.

Inhale: Prepare.

2 Exhale: Engage the core muscles and the obliques to imprint the pelvis. Think about drawing the tailbone to the floor.

Hold for 30 seconds. Repeat other side.

Imprint is the second position used for the pelvis in Pilates, a slight backward tilt, bringing the hip bones and pubic bone closer together. This is initiated by the obliques and rectus abdominus. Think of drawing the tailbone to the floor. Engage the buttocks to encourage the hip to open.

glute stretch

Focus: Glutei (buttocks).

1 Start position: Supine on the mat, neutral pelvis. One leg resting over the ball. Other leg bent with the foot resting on the knee of the leg on the ball.

Inhale: Prepare.

2 Exhale: Roll the ball toward you to feel a stretch in the buttocks.

Hold for 30 seconds. Repeat other side.

Once you can feel the stretch, make sure that you keep breathing to help the muscle release.

stretch and release | 89

how to put it together

Ideally, you will have time to complete a full workout including all the exercises but if you don't, use the following workout charts to put together a balanced workout. Try to vary your workout through the week so that you do each exercise at least once—don't just stick to your favorites! Make sure that you warm up and cool down properly.

Level 1

Pick one exercise from each section:

Warm-up	Flexion	Lumbar Flexion	Extension	Rotation
Breathing (page 24)	Ab Prep (legs over the ball) (page 44)	Roll Over Prep (page 54)	Breaststroke 1 (release with the Shell) (page 46)	Spine Twist (page 51)
Neutral (page 26)	Roll Up Prep (page 50)	Half Roll Back (page 49)		
Imprint and Release (page 29)	The Hundred (seated on the ball) (page 48)			
Hip Release (page 36)				
Spinal Rotation (page 37)				
Hip Rolls (page 38)				
Scapulae Isolations (page 32)				
Elevation and Depression (Shoulders) (page 33)				
Arm Circles (page 40)				
Chest Opener (page 41)				
Head Nods (page 31)				

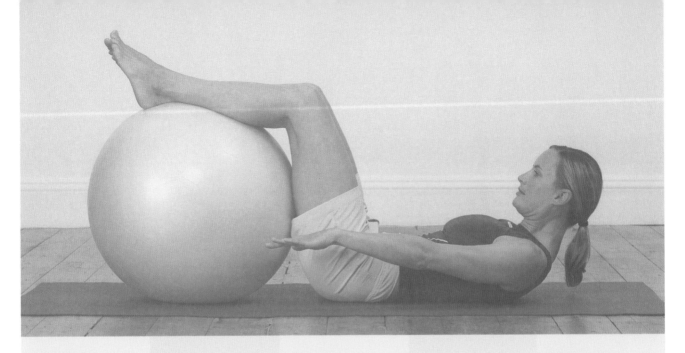

Hip/Legs

One Leg Circle
(*page 52*)

Single Leg Stretch
(*page 53*)

Single Leg Extension
(*page 56*)

Heel Squeeze Prone
(*page 55*)

Chest

Push-ups (hands on the ball) (*page 58*)

Scapulae Stability

Scapulae Stability (over the ball)
(*page 57*)

Lateral Flexion

Mermaid (*page 59*)

Stretch and Release

See chapter 7

Level 2

You will still be using some of the level 1 exercises as part of your level 2 workout. Remember that you can stay with the level 1 option for an exercise if it still challenges you; there is no rush to move on. Keep your workout balanced by choosing one exercise from each section and try to practice each exercise at least once per week. Make sure that you warm up and cool down properly.

Pick one exercise from each section:

Warm-up	Flexion	Lumbar Flexion	Extension	Rotation
Breathing (page 24)	Ab Prep (in supine bridge) (page 62)	Roll Over Prep (page 54)	Breaststroke 1 or 2 (release with the Shell) (pages 46 and 63)	Spine Twist (page 51)
Neutral (page 26)	Full Roll Up (page 65)	Half Roll Back (page 49)		Half Roll Back with Obliques (page 66)
Imprint and Release (page 29)	The Hundred (in supine incline) (page 64)			
Hip Release (page 36)				
Spinal Rotation (page 37)				
Hip Roll (page 38)				
Scapulae Isolations (page 32)				
Elevation and Depression (Shoulders) (page 33)				
Arm Circles (page 40)				
Chest Opener (page 41)				
Head Nods (page 31)				

Hip/Legs

One Leg Circle
(page 52)

Single Leg Stretch
(page 53)

Single Leg Extension
(page 56)

Heel Squeeze Prone
(page 55)

Side Leg Lift
(page 67)

Chest

Push-ups (over the ball) *(page 68)*

Balance

Seated Leg Lifts
(page 69)

Lateral Flexion

Mermaid with Rotation *(page 70)*

Stretch and Release

See chapter 7

Intermediate

Now that you are working at an intermediate level, try to work out for 45 minutes or an hour. Choose at least one exercise per section but more if you have time. You will include some of the level 2 exercises as part of your intermediate workout. Stay with the level 2 option for an exercise if it still challenges you. Make sure that you warm up and cool down properly.

Pick one exercise from each section:

Warm-up

Breathing *(page 24)*

Neutral *(page 26)*

Imprint and Release *(page 29)*

Hip Release *(page 36)*

Spinal Rotation *(page 37)*

Hip Roll *(page 38)*

Scapulae Isolations (seated) *(page 32)*

Elevation and Depression (Shoulders) *(page 33)*

Arm Circles *(page 40)*

Chest Opener *(page 41)*

Head Nods *(page 31)*

Flexion

Ab Prep (in supine bridge) *(page 62)*

Full Roll Up *(page 65)*

The Hundred (in supine bridge) *(page 64)*

Double Leg Stretch *(page 75)*

Lumbar Flexion

Roll Over Prep *(page 54)*

Half Roll Back *(page 49)*

Elephant *(page 79)*

Extension

Breaststroke 1 or 2 *(pages 46 and 63)*

Full Breaststroke (release with the Shell) *(page 76)*

Rotation

Spine Twist *(page 51)*

Half Roll Back with Obliques *(page 66)*

Hip/Legs

One Leg Circle
(hips lifted)
(page 74)

Side Leg Lift
(page 67)

Single Leg Stretch
(upper body flexed)
(page 53)

Chest

Push-ups (over the
ball, resting on shins)
(page 68)

Core

Leg Pull Front
(page 78)

Lateral Flexion

Mermaid with Chest
Opener (side twist)
(page 82)

Stretch and Release

See chapter 7

index